DEAR ABRAHAM,

This is your Channukah/
hristmas 2019 gift for
ourself. I remember, now
hat I'm alone, asking
ank if The Kabbalah
nter is going to be
ere for him if he gets
and almost dies, or if
y are going to help him
pe his ass when he gets

old, and his answer was: "No, and they're not supposed to be there for me."

The Zohar and The Red String Book offer/promise protection, just from owning them. Maybe one day, I will be able to understand better. For now, I'm still excited about Kabbalah, and I definitely believe. Although Frank left me, may be he'll come back. That was always my

opes for Yehuda, as well.
Good Luck healing..

- Abe

THE RED STRING BOOK

Distributed by Publishers Group West

THE RED STRING
BOOK

THE POWER OF PROTECTION

Technology for the Soul™

YEHUDA BERG

DEDICATION

I want to dedicate this book to the Chevre. You are more than my friends—you are my family.

Thank you for committing your life to making the world a better place, for caring for the needs of others before your own, for being at the front line of the army in the war against pain and suffering.

May you always be protected and shielded from harm's way.

I love you all.

For further information:

The Kabbalah Centre
155 E. 48th St., New York, NY 10017
1062 S. Robertson Blvd., Los Angeles, CA 90035

1.800.Kabbalah www.kabbalah.com

Revised Edition
January 2007
Printed in USA
ISBN 13: 978-1-57189-567-7
ISBN 10: 1-57189-567-1

Design: Hyun Min Lee (HL Design: www.hldesignco.com)

TABLE OF CONTENTS

ACKNOWLEDGMENTS

To the people who make my life better each and every day: my parents, the Rav and Karen; my brother Michael; my wife Michal and our children; and my dear friend Billy.

FOREWORD

If it were not for one particular weekend when I was talking to my good friend Michael Shane, this book would never have been written. Michael and I were talking, and suddenly an idea came to him. He said that without an actual book about the concept of the Red String, millions of people would never truly have the opportunity to benefit from this simple yet powerful tool. Thank you for the idea, Michael.

And were it not for Andy Behrman, who suddenly appeared in my life during the writing of this book, chances are most people would never know this book was even available. Andy has done so much for bringing the awareness of the Red String Book to the world. His effort will be felt for years to come. Andy was motivated by his own lifesaving experience with Kabbalah. He tasted this power in his life and realized that he had to share it with others.

It's funny—we never know who will come into our lives

at a particular time or why, but there is always a bigger plan at work. If we just allow ourselves to be open to all possibilities with a sincere mind and heart, and if we are prepared to listen to everyone who has something to say without judgment or our own agenda, we will constantly receive all the help we need to fulfill our destiny.

"The envious man thinks that if his neighbor breaks a leg, he will be able to walk better himself."
—Helmut Schoeck

INTRODUCTION

The Evil Eye? Come on. Is there really a negative force, a dangerous stream of energy that emanates from the eyes of another person? That's a good question. The answer can be found in an ancient body of wisdom that dates back more than 4,000 years, to the time of Abraham, the father of Judaism, Christianity, and Islam.

This body of ancient wisdom is called Kabbalah.

WHAT IS KABBALAH?

Imagine there was a miraculous source of power so profound and powerful that it could totally heal and transform one's life and genuinely change our world for the good—forever! According to the greatest sages of history, there is just such a force. It's called Kabbalah, and it is the oldest, most influential wisdom in the world.

WHAT KABBALAH IS NOT

The biggest misconception people have about Kabbalah is that it's some sort of religion. Completely false! Totally untrue. Kabbalah is not a religion. Kabbalah is about as religious as the laws of electricity. Kabbalah is a technology, and *Webster's Dictionary* defines technology as *"...the practical application of knowledge, especially in a particular area."*

The particular area for which Kabbalah provides practical knowledge is *life!*

In providing technology for the soul and for the welfare of human beings, Kabbalah suddenly becomes a source of universal wisdom and universal tools that can effect transformation and ignite fulfillment for all people, regardless of their race, religion, faith, or gender. Just as computer technology can be utilized by anyone, so too can Kabbalistic technology be harnessed by all who are in need of it. When one truly understands that we are dealing with technology and not religion, rites, or rituals, the power to change anything and everything becomes accessible to the world in a nonjudgmental and nondogmatic fashion. Let's explore this idea further.

In religion, certain repetitive actions are performed out of faith or tradition. In Kabbalah, actions are taken because of the knowledge of cause and effect. In other words, we know a specific act will produce a specific effect because that is exactly how the technology operates. There is no blind faith—only results. And if the results are not there, one would be foolish to continue with the same behavior.

When one is empowered with the technology that governs our soul and spiritual reality, one can attain knowledge about the technologies that work in our physical world. By the way, this is precisely how many of the greatest scientists of history "discovered" the laws of nature.

THE INFLUENCE OF KABBALAH

The renowned spiritual sages of antiquity were not alone in their belief that Kabbalah could transform the world. The greatest scientific minds of history held the same opinion. Sir Isaac Newton, Henry More (Newton's teacher), and physicist Wilhelm Leibniz (Newton's greatest competitor) all believed that Kabbalah was the *prisca theologia*. Scary Latin term? Not really. It means the "original wisdom," and the great physicists and philosophers of the scientific revolution were convinced that prisca theologia could reconcile science with spirituality and unify all the people of the world. It could transform the planet into paradise and bring about heaven on earth. This wisdom, according to Newton, was secretly given to Moses on Mount Sinai some 3,400 years ago.

Newton and his peers were convinced that Kabbalah was the purest source of this long-lost ancient original wisdom. Interestingly, Newton's greatest discoveries are also found inside ancient Kabbalistic manuscripts.

Coincidence? Doubtful. Scholarship and recent archeological discoveries show that Kabbalah was essentially the core teachings of Abraham, Moses, Jesus, Muhammad, Pythagoras, Plato, Shakespeare, Freud, and Jung.

The Promise of Kabbalah

Kabbalah unravels all the mysteries of the universe. In the process, it reveals the spiritual and physical laws that govern both the universe and the human soul. Kabbalah answers questions, provides solutions, unravels puzzles, and deciphers codes. It offers practical tools with which to effect authentic change in your life. It creates order out of chaos. And as if that weren't enough, Kabbalah answers the ultimate question of human existence: *Why are we here on this earth?*

Let's find out more.

GOD, ELVIS, AND THE MEANING OF YOUR EXISTENCE

You are on this earth for one reason only: You asked to be here. That's right—Kabbalah says that you, personally, asked to be placed within this dark physical world of chaos. Of course, you don't remember any of this. Think about it: If you can't remember life in your own mother's womb, how can you possibly recall your existence in the cosmic womb that preceded the creation of this world? Well, think of this chapter as your reminder.

Why Be Here?

So, why did you do it? Why did you want to leave the womb of paradise and enter this nasty world of obstacles? For one deeply important reason: so that you could experience what it means to be a creator. Put another way, instead of having endless paradise handed to you freely by your Creator, you desired something far better: the chance to have a hand in actually creating that endless paradise. In short, you wanted to become a proactive participant in the process of creation rather than remain a reactive bystander.

In other words, you decided that being Elvis is far better than being an Elvis impersonator.

HIDE AND SEEK

Here's another way to understand the reason for life on earth as you know it: You're ten years old. You and a bunch of kids get together for a fierce game of hide and seek. You're ready for some serious fun. Some real competition. The game starts and you're *It*. You cover your eyes. You begin counting to ten. You're juiced. Pumped. You reach ten. You open your eyes. But now you're taken aback. Why? Because everyone's standing right in front of you!

Are you happy? Not in the least.

Can the purpose of the game, which is to experience pleasure, be achieved? No way.

Even though you "found" all the kids, are you having fun? Of course not.

For you to receive pleasure, all the kids must hide. The effort of finding each individual kid is what makes this game so enjoyable, so worthwhile. The act of *hiding* is the mechanism that produces all the fun. This sounds like a simple concept, but its implications are infinitely profound.

THE GAME BEGINS

Before the existence of this physical world, all the souls of humanity dwelled in a reality far more authentic than this one. Kabbalah calls it the Endless World. All the joy and bliss you can imagine was yours in the Endless World. But you and all the souls of humanity asked the Creator to hide all of the bliss so you could also have the pleasure of finding it.

GOD HIDES, YOU SEEK!

As you can plainly see, God agreed. He said yes to your request. So God hid his Light, and in doing so he hid all the joy and infinite fulfillment that are your ultimate destiny. Now you have to go out and find that Light. But when you do find it, you and only you will be responsible for receiving it in your life. You will have become the cause and creator of your everlasting joy. And there you have the meaning of your existence:

To find the hidden truths of life.

To find the hidden Light that can fulfill your every desire.

To find the hidden God that is the source of all this Light.

To become the cause and creator of your paradise.

The next question is, how did God manage to hide everything?

THE CURTAIN

Kabbalah says the Creator hung up a big curtain. This curtain conceals the Light in the same way that a thick curtain blocks out sunlight from a room. In both cases, the Light never really disappears. The curtain merely conceals what's always there.

The problems you encounter in life do not occur because there is no Light; rather, chaos occurs because a curtain hides all the Light. According to Kabbalah, instead of praying to God to fulfill all your desires (as if an all-loving God would ever say no), you must simply remove the curtain. Once you do so, Light will automatically shine into your life.

That seems simple enough. But for some reason, it's really not.

THE POWER OF THE CURTAIN

Imagine being in a large, windowless room with just a single light source: a shining lamp. Now imagine that a piece of blackout curtain is draped over the lamp, and the room suddenly becomes pitch black. Think about this scenario for a moment. Because the room is totally dark, *you cannot see the curtain that's causing all this darkness.*

Do you see the problem? Simply by doing its job, the curtain not only manages to conceal the light but also conceals *itself* in the process. Consequently, you can't find the curtain, either. When you fully grasp this, you will have grasped the greatest secret of life. Which leads to the next step . . .

The Paradox of Life

So how can we possibly remove a curtain that we cannot even see in order to free ourselves from the darkness? The very darkness is preventing us from locating the cause of the darkness in the first place! We're caught in a Catch-22 situation. How do we break this vicious cycle?

IDENTIFYING THE CURTAIN

Long ago the ancient masters of Kabbalah identified the curtain that conceals the Light of the Creator. Are you ready to find out what has been keeping us in the dark for so many millennia? Get ready . . .

The curtain is the human ego.

There you have it, plain and simple. Now you know. And this curtain—ego—does such a good job of hiding all the Light, including your true self (your soul), that you have forgotten and lost touch with all the true desires that radiate from your innermost being. Instead, you are governed and ruled by the whims of ego. You work around the clock to fulfill its desires, no matter how shallow or self-destructive those desires may be. These egocentric impulses control us 99.999 percent of the time. And if you have a difficult time believing this to be true, the curtain is doing its job extremely well.

As a result, with the Light hidden, with our souls concealed, we flounder around in a world of darkness—one so dense that we can't even see the hidden cause of our problems.

Until now.

THE FABRIC OF EGO

The curtain called ego is a multilayered fabric, woven by every egocentric action and deed. The layers in this fabric include anger, jealousy, rage, jealousy, worry, jealousy, anxiety, jealousy, intolerance, jealousy, prejudice, jealousy, resentment, jealousy, frustration, jealousy, pessimism, jealousy, and selfishness.

Clearly, ego is the foundation of all forms of envy. It compels you to convince others that you're right even when you're wrong. Ego gives you the illusion that you act freely, but in reality you are captive to its desires. When ego expresses itself as envy, you're held hostage to constant pressure to outdo your friends and colleagues. You're in bondage to your reactive whims and self-absorbed desires. You're captive to your job and financial pressures. You're a prisoner to other people's perceptions of you. You're incarcerated by your need for other people's acceptance. You're in prison and you don't even know it.

Drawing Back the Curtain

You came to this world to triumph over and transform all these negative traits. Each time you identify a trait in a given circumstance and choose to let it go for good, you remove a layer of curtain. This means life gets a little better and a little brighter, or lighter. What's more, it also means you are the cause of this revelation of Light. Surprise! You've just fulfilled one part of the ultimate purpose of your life.

Conversely, each time you react with ego in a given situation, even when it's justified, you drape a layer of curtain over your soul and over the Light of the Creator. That means life grows a little bit darker.

THE POWER OF ANNOYANCES

Hopefully, by now you're beginning to realize why your life is filled with irritating people and annoying problems. It's because annoyances are a good thing. They trigger your ego so you can stop your reaction and eradicate these traits from your nature. All obstacles, both large and small, are really opportunities to find the Light. But here's the conundrum: You've been programmed and conditioned all of your life to despise obstacles and to steer clear of problems, never realizing what they really offer you. As a result, you focus your attention on your positive traits, and you completely ignore, constantly deny, or remain in the dark when it comes to your egocentric qualities. "If I'm such a good person," you ask, "why did all this chaos suddenly befall me?" Well, now you know the answer.

The Greatest Trick the Devil (Ego) Did Was Convincing the World He Didn't Exist

You did not come into this world to be rewarded or honored for your good traits. To the contrary, you came into this world to find the Light hiding behind your unpleasant traits. But, as previously stated, the ego is so effective at hiding the truth, you don't even recognize the truth of its existence or the role it plays in causing you so much pain and suffering.

The good news is that this book has just opened your eyes to what really matters in life: *the changing of your character*. However, the journey of transformation is a difficult one. That's why the Kabbalists gave you a few tools to help us navigate the world of chaos and facilitate the overthrow of your ego.

Dangerous Openings

One of these tools concerns protection from what is known as the Evil Eye.

You probably noticed that the most common (and most dangerous) trait on the list mentioned earlier is jealousy. When you react with this trait, you create a curtain. But jealousy has an additional side effect, and one that is uniquely unpleasant: Not only do you create a curtain, but you also create an opening. You create an opening for the jealous looks and envious stares that often arise from your enemies and even from your friends.

And that's an enormous problem.

A person possessed of an evil eye carries with him the eye of the destroying negative force; hence, such a person is called a "destroyer of the world." People should be on their guard against such a person and not come near them so that they should not be injured by them!

—The Zohar

THE EVIL EYE

If looks could kill...An icy stare...A murderous glance...A wicked glare.

Throughout human history, the eyes have been linked to all kinds of spiteful behavior and ill effects, often referred to as the Evil Eye. Upon hearing this term for the first time, many people react to it as if it were something from the Dark Ages, like witchcraft or sorcery. In fact, the concept of the Evil Eye is not only modern, it's realistic and profound. It refers to a powerful negative energy that constantly circulates in everyday life. Specifically, the Evil Eye is a code name for envy—that which ignites feelings of anger and resentment in so many people when they're confronted with another person's success or good fortune. This can take place either consciously or subconsciously.

The Evil Eye refers to the visual stream that flows from a person's eye as the result of a covetous stare or resentful glance accompanying well-intentioned or ill-intentioned words of praise. You may not realize it, but envious eyes and jealous looks have a tangible effect on your life and well-being. They can hold you back from achieving your full potential in every area of your life.

A BRIEF HISTORY OF THE EVIL EYE

In Italy, it's called *mal occhio*. Kabbalists refer to it as *ayin horeh*. Arabs pronounce it *ayin harsha*. The Scottish know it as *droch shuil*. And the Romans dubbed it *oculus malus*.

Whatever you choose to call it, the concept of the Evil Eye goes back thousands of years. The Evil Eye is mentioned in the Bible and is a phenomenon acknowledged by Muslims, Jews, and Christians. The giants of Greek philosophy—Socrates, Plato, and Aristotle—spoke of it as well. Moses wrote about it. Kings, queens, and presidents devised strategies to guard their nations against it. In fact, eye makeup originated in India as a tool to shield people from the negative visual stream caused by the Evil Eye. In ancient Egypt, eye shadow and lipstick were worn for the same purpose—to reflect away negative glances and envious stares. The Greeks often painted an eye near the bow of their battleships to ward off the Evil Eye, and ancient warriors once adorned their helmets and shields with flashy ornaments to neutralize evil forces emanating from the eyes of the opposing army.

THE EFFECTS OF THE EVIL EYE

The need to confront the negative influences of the Evil Eye should never be underestimated. Make no mistake, your ego will pipe in and tell you it's all superstition. But anyone who doesn't understand the Evil Eye's effects and fails to activate a protective shield against it will eventually become its victim. You'll begin to experience medical problems, such as backaches, colds, and the flu. You'll start having problems with your business, or a brutal fight in a personal relationship. The Evil Eye is a contributing factor to these and a host of other maladies. In fact, history's greatest spiritual sages and religious authorities attributed a majority of deaths to the Evil Eye. And all those tiny currents of doubt circulating in your mind right now exist only because your ego is a master at hiding spiritual truths from your conscious mind. Words like *myth*, *fairytale*, and *fallacy* are all born of ego.

You can be sure of this: Negative feelings are everywhere. You may not realize it, but very often even the people who have envious feelings are not consciously aware of them. But that doesn't make those feelings any less destructive. In fact, the camouflaged nature of the Evil Eye is one of its most dangerous attributes—not only for the targets of envious feelings, but also for the individuals in whom those feelings arise.

In short, the Evil Eye is a real danger with which you must contend in your everyday life, and the teachings of the great Kabbalists have always emphasized this. A verse in a Kabbalistic meditation even refers explicitly to the dangers posed by jealousy and envy: *"Let it be your will that you shall save me from an evil eye."*

JUDGMENT CAN NEVER, BUT NEVER, BEFALL YOU—UNLESS...

Here's a remarkable, profound spiritual truth and universal law: According to Kabbalah, your own actions, sins, and negative behavior can never come back to judge you. Your words and confessions can never inflict retribution upon you. The force called God cannot judge you. The cosmos will never penalize you. This is a rock-solid spiritual principle of life. It's pretty incredible, isn't it? And comforting, too.

How, then, do you invite so much judgment into your life?

To Cast an Evil Eye

Kabbalah says that the world is strategically arranged so that all the people in your life—from your closest friends to your most casual acquaintances, from your dearest family members to strangers who pass you on the street—share sins similar to your own. Here's how it happens: The sins and negative traits of others will be shown to you during the course of your daily life. The moment you choose to pass judgment on those traits, you have pulled the trigger on yourself. In other words, only your words, *when spoken against another*, can cause a guilty verdict to be rendered on you. Once you cast the Evil Eye on someone else, you open the door for the Evil Eye and the forces of reckoning to come upon you.

So, it's up to you to take care of yourself. It always will be.

Conversely, if you withhold judgment on a person, then judgment can never befall you. Imagine the possibilities. What a kind, merciful, and forgiving world you could inhabit if you just stopped judging others. Remember this before you judge.

What a secret—if you'd only known and grasped this universal law before! Well, the milk is already spilled, so it's important to move forward, put aside the pain you've endured in the past, and start focusing on the *now*. Make up your mind to neutralize your envy, defuse your jealousy, and put an end to all of your justified acts of judgment so you can protect yourself from your own nasty and dastardly deeds.

THE DYNAMICS OF THE EVIL EYE

The teachings of Kabbalah describe the actual mechanics of the Evil Eye in meticulous detail. Here's how it works.

When an envious look is directed at one person by another, a contraction takes place on the target victim's spiritual level of being. Specifically, the protective energy force that naturally surrounds a person, known as *mercy*, suddenly pulls back, leaving a void in its wake. Subsequently, an energy force known as *judgment* enters the void that's been created. The energy of judgment is a strange thing. It has one purpose and one sole function: to examine everything it encounters, strictly and without making any concessions.

For example, if someone looks with envy at the parents of a newborn baby, or the baby itself, the protective Light that surrounds the infant contracts. A void is created. The energy of judgment is then activated and fills that void. This scrutinizing force immediately begins to "check the balance books" and raise questions such as:

Why did these people receive such a wonderful, healthy baby?

This penetrating force will not stop until it finds faults, liabilities, and demerit points in the lives of these people, for that is its sole nature. That's all it knows how to do. And the moment it finds even the smallest infraction, judgments are free to flow to the child. Furthermore, as you learned previously, judgment is also directed against the person who initiated the envious glance in the first place. In essence, everyone loses. It's a classic no-win situation for all concerned.

Our envy of others devours us most of all.

—Aleksandr Solzhenitsyn (1918–)

WHERE ENVY LURKS

Envy is especially prevalent in today's high-pressure world, in which there's an overwhelming sense of competition and a need to be the best, the richest, the most successful. This atmosphere creates a great deal of insecurity—arousing in many people the sneaking suspicion that perhaps they're not doing as well as they should, or that maybe they're not making as big a splash as the next guy. If you live in an environment such as this and you're doing well, the sad truth is that many people will not be happy about your success. And you, in turn, aren't likely to be happy about the success of others. Talk about a vicious circle.

If someone consciously or subconsciously begrudges your good fortune, it's not necessarily his or her fault. It takes some hard spiritual work, often over the course of a lifetime, before you can experience the good fortune of others as if it were your own. You're in a vulnerable state when someone close to you succeeds. In fact, the closer you are, the more vulnerable you may be to feelings of jealousy or anger. It can happen to sisters or brothers or best friends. If you aspire to true prosperity, this kind of negative energy is something you definitely need to be aware of.

THE NEED FOR PROTECTION

Long ago, Kabbalah recognized the need for protection from the repercussions of a jealous heart and an envious eye. So the Kabbalists devised a powerful spiritual technology to accomplish this objective on many levels: first, to protect you from the envious looks of others; and second, to help you eliminate your own jealousy and the Evil Eye that you cast toward others. They called this technology the Red String.

THE RED STRING

Have you ever seen someone wearing a Red String around their left wrist and wondered why they were wearing it? Maybe it was the waitress at your favorite restaurant, your doctor, or even a small child. What exactly is this red string? When you ask, they tell you it's all about protection. "Protection?" you say. Read on.

The question is, can the power of spiritual protection actually be transmitted through a simple strand of wool, colored red, worn on one's left wrist 24 hours a day, seven days a week? Then again, you might also ask, can movies and television shows actually be transmitted through a simple strand of copper wire, connected to the back of a television set, 24 hours a day, seven days a week? The answer to both questions is a resounding yes! Spiritual and physical technologies both work the same way.

THE POWER OF RED

Red strings, red blood on the doorposts, and red wine are all mentioned in the Bible in connection with the idea of protection against the forces of death and destruction. Red is a significant color for a number of reasons. It has the lowest frequency on the color spectrum, signifying the lowest level of light or extreme negativity. You're probably wondering, why would you use the most negative color and the lowest frequency of spiritual energy to protect yourself from the forces of negativity?

Think about a polio vaccine, or a vaccination against whooping cough or any other dreaded disease. When you receive an inoculation against a particular illness, a weakened strain of the actual disease is integrated into the vaccine. Spiritual immunizations work in much the same way. The color red injected into the wool string is a diluted strain of negative energy. Thus, it vaccinates you from the destructive negative forces of the Evil Eye. Yes, it's that simple.

WHY WOOL?

According to Kabbalah, two opposing forces of mercy and judgment permeate the world. According to The Zohar, the world "spins with judgment and spins with mercy." Pain occurs when there's too much judgment in your life and not enough mercy. When you combine the two, judgment is automatically converted into mercy because mercy is thus the only true reality—the light beneath the curtain.

Let's examine this concept further by way of an analogy. Consider a dark room with an unlit lamp. The darkness corresponds to the force of judgment. The potential light from the lamp corresponds to the force of mercy. Whenever you combine light and darkness, by flipping on the light switch, something profound occurs: The darkness converts into light. *But the reverse never takes place!* Light is never converted into darkness.

The Power of Light

Consider the following: No matter how large a dark room is, even if it's the size of five football fields, a single candle will convert a portion of the darkness into light. But if a single candle is shining in a tiny room and you increase the amount of darkness in the room by expanding it tenfold, the added darkness has no effect whatsoever on the light. Light always disrupts and converts darkness. But darkness is powerless in the presence of light. This deeply important principle is mirrored in the spiritual world and is the technology underlying the Red String.

Though they be like red crimson, they shall be as white as wool . . . All the judgments become whitened.
—The Zohar

Though your sins be like scarlet, they shall be as white as snow.
—The Zohar

THE POWER OF WOOL

Everything in this world is a reflection of either the force of mercy or the force of judgment. For example, white blood cells in your body correspond to mercy. They are integral to your immune system, giving you a defense against disease (judgment). They fight infections, create antibodies to attack invaders, and provide emergency care to injuries by clotting. Red blood cells, on the other hand, correspond to the force of judgment. If a knife cuts a person, red blood (judgment) is spilled. White blood cells then respond by clotting (mercy) to stop the bleeding.

Long ago, in The Zohar, Kabbalists categorized the entire physical world, describing the energetic root of every form of matter in the material realm. Linen, for example, embodies the force of judgment. Wool, on the other hand, embodies the force of mercy. The color white reflects the energy of mercy, while the color red reflects the frequency of judgment.

By dyeing white wool (mercy) red (judgment), you physically create the wiring that converts judgment to mercy or darkness into Light. This is the process that takes place with the Red String. In truth, the string is actually white, not red. That's right; it's pure white wool. But the color red is used to attract and intercept all forces of judgment streaming from the Evil Eye, binding it to the string. Now the transformed white wool string converts judgment into mercy, and you receive your protection.

STRING THEORY

As you can see, the Red String allows you not only to remove negative influences, but also to transform those influences into their spiritual opposite. In this way, even the energy of the Evil Eye can change from a channel for negativity into a profoundly healing form of energy. That's how the string operates.

But wearing the string is not a 100 percent substitute for spiritual work and protection. You must always be cognizant of the reason you're on this earth. Oh, you forgot already? I hope not. Never forget it: You came here to pull back the curtains that conceal the Light. Those curtains are your negative traits. The more you work at identifying and banishing all of your ruthless attributes, especially jealousy, the more powerful the Red (white) String will prove to be.

Activating the String

The Red String technology, developed by the sages of Kabbalah, begins in Israel with the winding of Red

String around the tomb of Rachel, the matriarch of the Bible. Rachel is considered by kabbalists to be the mother of the world, and her greatest desire is to protect and defend all of her children from evil. A mother's natural protective love is perhaps the mightiest power in all existence. Consequently, connecting the Red String to Rachel charges it with the forces of love and protection.

After being wrapped around Rachel's tomb a prescribed number of times, the Red String is cut into pieces and worn on the left wrist. Why not the right wrist? As you've learned, everything in the world is rooted in either positive or negative energy, judgment or mercy, receiving or sharing. The left arm and hand pertain to the concept of receiving. The right arm and hand embody the force of imparting. Consequently, negative forces headed your way enter your body's system through the left side. By wearing the Red String on your left wrist, you intercept, defuse, and convert any negative forces right at the front gate, their precise point of entry. It's important to note that anyone can wear the Red String; they don't necessarily have to be studying Kabbalah.

Wearing the Red String

Just before putting on the string, you should ask for the strength and consciousness to always radiate compassion, kindness, and forgiveness toward everyone you meet, and to always feel a deep sense of appreciation for everything you have in your life, *right now*, so you never have to cast a jealous eye toward another human being. Next, it is advisable to ask someone whom you trust, respect, and, ideally, love—as well as someone with whom you have a "connection"—to tie the Red String to your left wrist.

First, have them tie the string closely around your wrist with a simple knot. Then have them repeat the gesture by knotting the string six more times for a total of seven knots. These seven knots signify white light (mercy), which contains the seven colors of the rainbow. (They also signify the seven spiritual worlds that influence reality.) Now make a promise to yourself that you will do your utmost to refrain from negative thoughts or gossip about others, no matter how deliciously tempting it may be. As this person ties the string to your left wrist, he or she will say a prayer against the Evil Eye.

What If My Red String Falls Off?

Some have asked, "If I wear my Red String for a few months and it naturally falls off, first, why does it happen, and second, what do I do?" The answer is simple: The Red String has done its job if it falls off over time, and there's no reason to panic. Have another Red String tied to your left wrist in the same way you had the first one tied. However, if this Red String falls off after a few days, there may be reason to examine your energy and your behavior toward others.

Keep Your Head Low

In addition to wearing the string, you should also wear the garment of humility. For example, don't speak too freely about your successes, because in doing so you make yourself a target for others. Again, this doesn't mean that people are all bad; it's simply human nature operating in the material realm. Also remember that while it may feel pretty darn good to boast and brag about your success, the pleasure you derive from doing so will probably last all of ten minutes. By contrast, the effects of the Evil Eye that flashiness attracts could last ten days, ten months, or even ten years. So don't be humble and low-key for moral or ethical reasons. Do it out of self-interest!

LOOKS CAN KILL

You've heard the saying, "If looks could kill." Well, as you've already discovered, a look filled with the resentment and envy of another person really *can* kill on a spiritual level. It can kill the joy and fulfillment that every human being really deserves from life.

As damaging as it is to receive an angry glance, giving one is even more destructive. When you do so, your own defenses are weakened in exact proportion to your negative feelings toward someone else. Understanding this principle *and living it* protects you not only from other people's harmful intentions, but also from your own. Keep this in mind each and every day if you want to empower that strand of red wool dangling from your left wrist.

Here are a few other "life" suggestions for bolstering the power of the Red String.

UNCONDITIONAL LOVE

Judicial robes are "one size fits all." They're easy to slip into, they're comfortable, and when you look in the mirror they make you seem very powerful and distinguished. It's always fun to don your robe and impose judgment on those around you. But it's also diametrically opposed to your own best interests.

As long as your human interactions are dominated by judgment and hostile evaluations, you yourself will be judged. As long as negative energy dominates your interactions, the Light you can receive is limited accordingly. Only by shedding your judicial robes, only by offering love without limits to everyone—whether they "deserve" it or not—can you gain joy and fulfillment that are also without limits.

The Light of fulfillment is there for you all the time, every day and every night, regardless of whether you're being "bad" or "good." The force we call the Creator sees you at your worst moments and still emanates unconditional love. If you can emulate that divine attribute—by offering love everywhere, without reason—you'll receive it in return. Always remind yourself of this vital insight. Each time you put on a new Red String, tell yourself:

My love is unconditional. It is its own reward.
I remove the labels of "friend" or "enemy" from the
people in my life, and extend my love to everyone.

UNITY

The negative forces in the world (ego) seek to create anger and discord between people. Unfortunately, that's not very difficult to do. Whether it's a dispute about who pays the bills, who's first in the checkout line, or who controls the TV remote, there's always an ample supply of things to argue about. Until you're able to turn away from all that, you'll never see true joy and fulfillment—either in your life or in the world.

One of the most dangerous things about anger is the way there always seems to be such a good excuse for it. You've been wronged, you've been hurt, you've been victimized—you've got every justification in the world for taking out your feelings on those responsible for your injustice. The only trouble is when you do so, you ensure the continuation of chaos and negativity everywhere.

Always ask for the power to see beyond surface conflicts to the deeper unity of all people. Seeing the unity will fill your eyes with love instead of envy.

RESISTING REACTIONS

Your eyes can shift from love to hate, serenity to jealousy, in an instant. This happens every time you react to a given situation. The key to controlling your glances is found in a concept called *resistance*. Namely, you resist the desire to react to instinctive impulses. Not only does this action of resistance prevent you from casting angry or jealous eyes at another person, it also helps you achieve your purpose in life.

How?

The moment you resist a reactive egocentric response, you find your true self—a proactive soul. That means you find the Light and fulfillment in that specific circumstance. When you react, you are not a creator. You are simply an effect. The person or situation that caused you to react is the cause. But when you resist reactions, you are now the cause of your emotion and the creator of your consciousness. That means fulfillment is now free to flow to you. You just won a round of hide and seek.

This, by the way, is the secret to getting all your prayers answered.

WHY PRAYERS GO UNANSWERED

Consider the following thought experiment. Suppose the electrical current in the walls of a large auditorium is analogous to the Light of God. Imagine yourself standing in the middle of this massive auditorium in complete darkness. You begin praying to the electricity to bring light to the room. You're sincere in your supplications. Pure of heart in your prayers. But does it matter? Will your heartfelt prayers turn on the lights?

Suppose you try to strike a deal with the electricity. You promise to worship it. You'll even erect a small temple inside the auditorium to honor it. You'll write scrolls of parchment whose words praise this unseen force and speak of it in story and parable.

Will these actions turn on the light?

Of course not.

The fact is, in order to generate an illumination; you

must walk over to the light switch and flip it on. Only then can "let there be light" manifest throughout the auditorium.

Herein lies the secret to activating the prayers of humankind. The Light of the Creator is ever-present and willing to fulfill your every need and desire.

Moreover, all the temples of the world, all the religions of human civilization, all the various prayers of humankind are akin to the lamps, lanterns, floodlights, and spotlights that can illumine the world.

But what about the actual switch that activates your prayers?

The actual light switch is your own behavior. The moment you apply the concept of resistance in your life, it's akin to flipping on the Light.

- You must resist your desire to blame others

- You must resist your urge to one-up and outdo your friends and foes

- You must resist your impulse to take it all for yourself, and instead, share a hefty-sized portion with others.

- You must resist your doubts about the truth of the Creator—especially when no one is looking.

- You must resist the impulse of envy and not cast the Evil Eye at your best friends or worst enemies.

This is how you turn on the switch. This is how *you* (not God) answer your own prayers!

APPRECIATION

For many people, the expectations of a better future translate into discontent with the here and now. Once this viewpoint takes root, however, the feeling that you're being deprived in the present means the abundance you're waiting for will never really arrive—because you'll always be looking over the horizon toward what's next or what's more.

Always make an attempt to arouse certainty of joy and fulfillment in the future along with true happiness in what has *already* been given to you. This not only ensures that you will receive all that the Creator intends for you, but also brings protection from painful losses right now. "Use it or lose it" is an important Kabbalistic principle—and the best use of the Creator's gifts begins with sincere appreciation. If you take your health, your family and friends, and your financial security for granted, you give the negative forces an opportunity to place all those things in jeopardy.

Don't learn the importance of appreciation the hard way! Repeat these words of wisdom to yourself whenever you feel yourself lacking or coveting someone else's possessions:

> Just as I am certain that my life
> will be filled with abundance in the future,
> so do I appreciate what I have right now.

ACCOUNTABILITY

Bad things happen to good people. Or do they? Kabbalah teaches you to remove the moral labels from the events of your life. This doesn't mean that the actions of criminals and dictators are benign or ethically neutral. Rather, it means that focusing on rightness or wrongness will not get you where you need to go on a spiritual level. By the same token, blame—even when the facts seem to justify it—can only corrode your inner being.

So, what's the alternative to "when bad things happen"? It's easy to say, but not easy to put into action. Very simply, the alternative is to *accept responsibility*. Know that the world operates on a cause-and-effect basis, and recognize that nothing happens by chance. For everything that happens in your life, there is a cause—and you are it! Whatever happens to you may be the result of a negative action you did ten minutes ago, ten days ago, ten months ago, ten years ago, or even ten lifetimes ago.

Once again, you may not find this easy to accept, but doing so is the only way to truly take control of your own destiny and to grasp the joy and fulfillment that are its essence. Remember, it is only the ego that implants all these doubts and uncertainties that you have about these spiritual truths. So transcend the ego and tell yourself this:

I am never a victim.
I am responsible for everything that happens in
my life—and for understanding that it happens
for the best.

If you can live your life in harmony with all these Kabbalistic insights, your Red String (and your behavior) will protect you in ways you cannot even imagine.

STRINGS IN STORES:
THE CONTROVERSY

Ever since the Red String first began appearing on the public scene a few years ago, a small faction of individuals within the religious community have opposed it, condemned it, and belittled it. Some have said that it's disgraceful to sell Red Strings in mainstream stores. Others have denounced the whole idea of selling Kabbalah to the masses. They say that Kabbalah should be reserved for the pious, the holy, and the spiritually mature. Well, the kabbalists of history say "rubbish"!

The famed 16th-century Moroccan Kabbalist, Abraham Azulai, predicted that in our very day, religion would become so corrupted, and the world would be so overcome with darkness and suffering, that it would be necessary to bring the wisdom of Kabbalah to the masses—especially to those who are turned off by organized religion. In response, the eminent kabbalists of history declared that we should put Kabbalah out in the public marketplace, making it simple and practical for all people. After all, everyone is entitled to receive blessings and protection in their lives. The kabbalists agreed and thus encouraged the dissemination of Kabbalah out in the market, where everyone could have access to it, rather than hiding it away in libraries and schools of religious learning. My father's own teacher, the great Kabbalist Rav Yehuda Brandwein, once said that if some people can market "lies" and "negativity" with slick promotion and cutting-edge package design, we should never feel ashamed about doing the same with spiritual truths! I personally believe that the great kabbalists of history would rather see the Red String and Kabbalah books in retail stores, where they can genuinely help and inspire people, than see video games that openly promote violence. Think about it. What's so wrong about selling a product in a store that teaches us not to be jealous of others, promotes tolerance, and provides protection at the same time? Nothing more need be said.

AND FINALLY

At the outset of this book, you learned that you and all the souls of humanity chose to play this game of life, a kind of cosmic game of hide and seek, so you could become the cause and creator of your own happiness. This game, though illusionary, is profoundly serious nonetheless. It's a game so well orchestrated and designed that you don't even realize you're playing a game 99 percent of the time. And it's a game that includes life and death, pleasure and pain, serenity and sadness.

When you play this game according to the life strategies presented throughout this book, you become immune to negativity. By incorporating unconditional love, accountability, appreciation, resistance, and unity into your life, you fortify your consciousness and empower your Red String. Developing a strong and positive state of mind protects you from potential chaos and, most important, from either giving or receiving jealous glances, envious stares, or looks of ill will.

What's more, when your spiritual energy field is strong, you ignite the power of transformation from judgment to mercy that is woven in the string. Each new round in this game called life becomes filled with ever increasing joy, order, kindness, and fulfillment.

Okay. So now it's time to get back to the game.

You're *It*.

Close your eyes.

Count to ten.

And go find all the fulfillment that is your ultimate destiny.

Ready?

Go!

AFTERWORD

Now that you've learned the basics of the ancient wisdom of Kabbalah and discovered the amazing power of protection available to you in the Red String, it's time to put that new-found knowledge to work and begin to improve your life. Sit quietly with pen and paper or at the computer and approach the exercises that follow with honesty and sincere introspection. Take your time; you may need to revisit the questions several times or go back and re-read sections of the book. If you should find that envy is too overwhelming a force in your life and is blocking you from being able to complete the exercises on your own, you can find assistance at any time by calling 1-800-KABBALAH. An instructor will be happy to go through the exercises with you and help you with any questions you might have. Let's get started.

Exercise #1:

Make a list of people you envy. Be honest with yourself. What do they have that you think you are lacking? Do you think so-and-so is better looking than you are? More successful? Has a better relationship? A bigger home? Do you think they're spiritually "higher" than you?

Are you angry or resentful about their good fortune?

Were you aware of your feelings of envy before writing this list? Are the people you've listed aware of your feelings about them?

Think about the way in which jealousy contributes another layer to the curtain that hides the Light. What would you rather have, the things you're jealous of or more Light in your life?

Exercise #2:

Make a list of the people you think may be jealous of you. Have they made comments to you that would indicate their envy? Are you aware of them sending the negative energy of The Evil Eye in your direction? Can you feel how you are affected by the jealousy and envious looks of others?

What do you have that could create envy in others? Are you comfortable with people praising you? Do you tend to boast or brag or have you made a commitment to practice humility?

Exercise #3:

Imagine seeing yourself on a giant TV screen. You're watching yourself talking to someone who has something or some quality that makes you jealous. Every time you find yourself about to make a comment that reflects your envy, hit the pause button on your remote control. Wait a second. Resist the urge to speak before you think. Stop and ask yourself, *Do I really want to say what's about to come out of my mouth? Am I about to give this person the Evil Eye and bring judgment upon myself?*

After all, if you're not aware of what you're doing, how are you supposed to change it?

Exercise #4:

Take a good look at your life. Do you live/work/study in a highly competitive environment? Do you feel that you have to be the best? The richest? The thinnest? Does the success of others make you unhappy? Do you judge them harshly? Do you feel like a victim of bad luck or rotten circumstances?

Now write down all the things in your life that you're thankful for. Do you ever stop to appreciate what you already have? Do you take responsibility for being the cause of all that happens to you—the hard stuff as well as the good stuff you've earned through your own efforts?

Exercise #5:

We know that the Red String is a very powerful spiritual technology that protects us against jealous hearts and envious eyes—our own, as well as others. Think about the Red String and the way the white wool (mercy), when it is dyed red (judgment), deflects the negative energy of judgment and transforms it into a healing energy.

Now write down how you can convert judgment within you to mercy. In other words, how do you lift the curtain so your inner darkness turns into Light? (Hint: Reread the section about Resisting Reactions.)

Exercise #6:

The red wool for the Red String is wound around the tomb of Rachel, who is called the Mother of the World. Her greatest desire is to protect her children, so the string becomes imbued with the force of her love and protection.

What is so extraordinary about a mother's unconditional love? The ability to see beyond surface differences to the unity we all share as children of the universal Creator—to love ALL her children, even you.

Sit with this thought and receive the love of the Mother of the World. Can you feel your unity with all people, despite your differences?

Do you still feel envious of others?

For more information on the Red String and other technologies for the soul, please visit www.72.com—the official site of national best selling author Yehuda Berg—and discover the oldest technology in the world for affecting genuine transformation.

To facilitate the sharing of this important wisdom and its various tools, an outreach program was developed to give away Red Strings to children throughout the world who need it but cannot afford or access it. This program will also share Red Strings with families and other people who are at risk or in need of protection. The proceeds from the sale of this book support that program.

When you purchased the Red String book, you not only learned about an effective way to protect yourself but contributed to the distribution of the Red String to tens of thousands of children in the four corners of the world. For more information on how to be part of this amazing outreach program, go to www.72.com.

If you were inspired by this book in any way and would like to know how you can continue to enrich your life through the power of Kabbalah, here is what you can do next: Read the book *The Power of Kabbalah*.

The Power of Kabbalah

Imagine your life filled with unending joy, purpose, and contentment. Imagine your days infused with pure insight and energy. This is *The Power of Kabbalah*. It is the path from the momentary pleasure that most of us settle for, to the lasting fulfillment that is yours to claim. Your deepest desires are waiting to be realized. But they are not limited to the temporary rush from closing a business deal, the short-term high from drugs, or a passionate sexual relationship that lasts only a few short months.

Wouldn't you like to experience a lasting sense of wholeness and peace that is unshakable, no matter what may be happening around you? Complete fulfillment is the promise of Kabbalah. Within these pages, you will learn how to look at and navigate through life in a whole new way. You will understand your purpose and how to receive the abundant gifts waiting for you. By making a critical transformation from a reactive to a proactive being, you will increase your creative energy, get control of your life, and enjoy new spiritual levels of existence. Kabbalah's ancient teaching is rooted in the perfect union of the physical and spiritual laws already at work in your life. Get ready to experience this exciting realm of awareness, meaning, and joy.

The wonder and wisdom of Kabbalah has influenced the world's leading spiritual, philosophical, religious, and scientific minds. Until today, however, it was hidden away in ancient texts, available only to scholars who knew where to look. Now after many centuries, *The Power of Kabbalah* resides right here in this one remarkable book. Here, at long last is the complete and simple path—actions you can take right now to create the life you desire and deserve.

The Red String

The authentic red string, blessed at the site of Rachel's Tomb, this package includes enough for 4-5 uses. For description and how to wear, please review String Theory, page 62.

You can order these products from our Web site or by calling Student Support.

Student Support: Trained instructors are available 18 hours a day. These dedicated people are willing to answer any and all questions about Kabbalah and help guide you along in your effort to learn more. Just call **1-800-kabbalah**.

MORE PRODUCTS THAT CAN HELP YOU BRING THE WISDOM OF KABBALAH INTO YOUR LIFE

The Living Kabbalah System™: Out of the Darkness™

Take Your Life to the Next Level™ with this step-by-step, 23-day system for transforming your life and achieving lasting fulfillment.

This revolutionary interactive system incorporates the latest learning strategies, addressing all three learning styles:

- Auditory (recorded audio sessions)

- Visual (workbook with written concepts and graphics)

- Tactile (written exercises, self-assessments, and physical tools)

The sturdy carrying case makes the system easy and convenient to use, in the car, at the gym, on a plane, wherever and whenever you choose. Learn from today's great Kabbalah leaders—Kabbalistic scholar Yehuda Berg and Instructor Jamie Greene—in an intimate, one-on-one learning atmosphere. You get practical, actionable tools and exercises to integrate the wisdom of Kabbalah into your daily life.

In just 23 days you can learn to live with greater intensity, be more successful in business and relationships, and achieve your dreams. Why wait? Take your life to the next level starting today.

The 72 Names of God: Technology for the Soul™
By Yehuda Berg

The story of Moses and the Red Sea is well known to almost everyone; it's even been an Academy Award –winning film. What is not known, according to the internationally prominent author Yehuda Berg, is that a state-of-the-art technology is encoded and concealed within that biblical story. This technology is called the 72 Names of God, and it is the key—your key—to ridding yourself of depression, stress, creative stagnation, anger, illness, and other physical and emotional problems. In fact, the 72 Names of God is the oldest, most powerful tool known to mankind—far more powerful than any 21st century high-tech know-how when it comes to eliminating the garbage in your life so that you can wake up and enjoy life each day. Indeed, the 72 Names of God is the ultimate pill for anything and everything that ails you because it strikes at the DNA level of your soul.

The power of the 72 Names of God operates strictly on a soul level, not a physical one. It's about spirituality, not religiosity. Rather than being limited by the differences that divide people, the wisdom of the Names transcends humanity's age-old quarrels and belief systems to deal with the one common bond that unifies all people and nations: the human soul.

The 72 Names of God for Kids
By Yehuda Berg, with Dev Ross

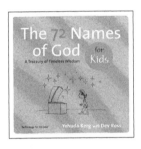

Charming color reproductions of original paintings by "At Risk" children are paired with simple stories, lessons, and meditations, to help children with specific issues and teach them how to make positive choices throughout their lives. This inspiring book with its timeless philosophy provides a way for children of all ages to gain a deeper understanding of their innate spiritual selves and find self-esteem, true friendship, love, and light.

Other titles in Yehuda Berg's *Technology for the Soul*™ Series:

Kabbalah On Love has a simple yet profound message: Love is not something you learn or acquire but an essence within, waiting to be revealed. Buried by layers of ego, fear, shame, doubt, low self-esteem, and other limitations, the incredibly powerful force that is love can only be activated by sharing and serving unconditionally.

Beyond Blame advocates taking personal responsibility instead of blaming and being a victim or martyr, through personal stories and simple exercises to help anyone overcome these negative tendencies and live a happier life.

God Does Not Create Miracles, You Do! gives the formula for removing obstacles to happiness by connecting to the true source of miracles within us.

The Monster Is Real tells us how to face our fears and eliminate them forever.

The Dreams Book shows how to use dream interpretation to find soul mates, discover career opportunities, prevent illness and develop awareness.

The Kabbalah Book of Sex
By Yehuda Berg

Much more than a sex manual, *The Kabbalah Book of Sex* reveals how to achieve real satisfaction, sexual pleasure, and the true fulfillment of desire through the secrets of Kabbalah. Most books about sex tend to focus on only one aspect: the physical mechanics. According to Kabbalah, the key to fulfilling sex lies in self-awareness, not simply technique. This provocative and stimulating book teaches how to overcome shame and lack of self-respect, how to access higher levels of connection—to ourselves, our partners, and to spirit—and how to make great sex last. Through the ancient wisdom of Kabbalah, the floodgates of passion and desire are endlessly opened, and light flows freely into every aspect of our lives.

God Wears Lipstick
By Karen Berg

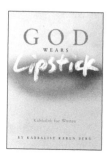

For millennia, the spiritual science known as Kabbalah has not only been skewed towards men and their issues, but women have literally been forbidden to study it. In this ground-breaking book, Karen Berg removes these barriers for the first time by revealing what was once taboo—Kabbalah for women. She provides an introduction to the basic principles of Kabbalah, with an emphasis on the special role that women play in the spiritual scheme of things, especially in the area of relationships. Also available, ***God Wears Lipstick Card Deck***, with the essence of the book distilled into simple meditations, in an attractive box of 72 cards.

Becoming Like God
By Michael Berg

At the age of 16, Kabbalistic scholar Michael Berg began the herculean task of translating *The Zohar*, Kabbalah's chief text, from its original Aramaic into its first complete English translation. *The Zohar*, which consists of 23 volumes, is considered a compendium of virtually all information pertaining to the universe, and its wisdom is only beginning to be verified today.

During the ten years he worked on *The Zohar*, Michael Berg discovered the long-lost secret for which mankind has searched for more than 5,000 years: how to achieve our ultimate destiny. *Becoming Like God* reveals the transformative method by which people can actually break free of what is called "ego nature" to achieve total joy and lasting life.

Berg puts forth the revolutionary idea that for the first time in history, an opportunity is being made available to humankind: an opportunity to Become Like God.

The Secret
By Michael Berg

Like a jewel that has been painstakingly cut and polished, *The Secret* reveals life's essence in its most concise and powerful form. Michael Berg begins by showing you how our everyday understanding of our purpose in the world is literally backwards. Whenever there is pain in our lives—indeed, whenever there is anything less than complete joy and fulfillment—this basic misunderstanding is the reason.

The Essential Zohar
By Rav Berg

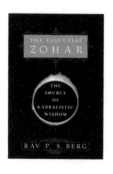

The Zohar has traditionally been known as the world's most esoteric and profound spiritual document, but Kabbalist Rav Berg, this generation's greatest living Kabbalist, has dedicated his life to making this wisdom universally available. The vast wisdom and Light of *The Zohar*

came into being as a gift to all humanity, and *The Essential Zohar* at last explains this gift to the world.

Wheels of a Soul
By Rav Berg

In *Wheels of a Soul*, Kabbalist Rav Berg reveals the keys to answering these and many more questions that lie at the heart of our existence as human beings. Specifically, Rav Berg explains why we must acknowledge and explore the lives we have already lived in order to understand the life we are living today . . .

Make no mistake: *you have been here before.* Reincarnation is a fact—and just as science is now beginning to recognize that time and space may be nothing but illusions, Rav Berg shows why death itself is the greatest illusion of all.

In this book you learn much more than the answers to these questions. You will understand your true purpose in the world and discover tools to identify your life's soul mate. Read *Wheels of a Soul* and let one of the greatest kabbalistic masters of our time change your life forever.

Power of You
By Rav Berg

For the past 5,000 years, neither science nor psychology has been able to solve the fundamental problem of chaos in people's lives.

Now, one man is providing the answer. He is Kabbalist Rav Berg.

Beneath the pain and chaos that disrupts our lives, Kabbalist Rav Berg brings to light a hidden realm of order, purpose, and unity. Revealed is a universe in which mind becomes master over matter—a world in which God, human thought, and the entire cosmos are mysteriously interconnected.

Join this generation's premier kabbalist on a mind-bending journey along the cutting edge of reality. Peer into the vast reservoir of spiritual wisdom that is Kabbalah, where the secrets of creation, life, and death have remained hidden for thousands of years.

THE KABBALAH CENTRE
The International Leader in the Education of Kabbalah

Since its founding, the Kabbalah Centre has had a single mission: to improve and transform people's lives by bringing the power and wisdom of Kabbalah to all who wish to partake of it.

Through the lifelong efforts of Kabbalists Rav and Karen Berg, and the great spiritual lineage of which they are a part, an astonishing 4 million people around the world have already been touched by the powerful teachings of Kabbalah. And each year, the numbers are growing!

I dedicate this book to Pinchas ben Issa,
Lisa bat Avraham, and Avraham ben Pinchas.

May spreading the wisdom of Kabbalah
bring certainty and trust in the Light,
and may all people share the fulfillment of
unity, peace, abundance, and joy.